Upcycling C

4th Edition

100 Upcycling Projects That Reuse Old Clothes to Create Modern Fashion Accessories, Trendy New Clothes & Home Décor!

by Kitty Moore

Copyright © 2017 By Kitty Moore
All rights reserved. No part of this book may be reproduced in any form without permission in writing from the author. No part of this publication may be reproduced or transmitted in any form or by any means, mechanic, electronic, photocopying, recording, by any storage or retrieval system, or transmitted by email without the permission in writing from the author and publisher.
For information regarding permissions write to author at kitty@artscraftsandmore.com.
Reviewers may quote brief passages in review.

Please note that credit for the images used in this book go to the respective owners. You can view this at: ArtsCraftsAndMore.com/image-list

Kitty Moore
ArtsCraftsAndMore.com

Table of Contents

Introduction	*8*
Clothes & Fashion Accessories	*9*
1. Turn Pants into Capris	*9*
2. Ombre Four-Strand Head Wrap	*10*
3. Cat Printed Jeans	*11*
4. Indigo Tie-Dye Jeans	*12*
5. Ombre Jeans with Bleach	*14*
6. Boyfriend Jeans	*16*
7. Jeans from Carrie Bradshaw	*17*
8. Lace Jeans	*18*
9. Peplum Top	*19*
10. Lace Scarf from An Old Table Cloth & T-Shirt	*21*
11. T-Shirt Wrap Skirt	*22*
12. Cute Ruffled T-Shirt	*23*
13. T-Shirt Dress	*25*
14. Shirt to Dress Upcycle	*26*
15. One Shoulder T-Shirt	*27*
16. Side Laced-Up DIY T-Shirt	*28*
17. Bleach-Dipped Aztec Jeans	*29*
18. Jeans with Patches	*30*
19. The Splatter-Paint Trend	*31*
20. Sexy Cut Up Leggings	*32*
21. Dip Dyed Pleated Skirt	*33*
22. Ruffle Necktie Tee	*34*

23. DIY No Knit Scarf _____ 35
24. Buttoned Up Infinity Scarf _____ 36
25. Re-Styled T-Shirt with Socks _____ 37
26. Woven Top _____ 38
27. T Shirt to Ruffled Dress _____ 39
28. Cool Summer Fringe Top _____ 40
29. Workout T-Shirt _____ 41
30. T-Shirt Twirly Skirt _____ 42
31. Tote Bag _____ 43
32. No Sew Crop Top! (With Hemming Option) _____ 45
33. No-Sew Cardigan _____ 46
34. No-Sew T-Shirt Bow Sleeves _____ 47
35. Men's Shirt into A Handbag _____ 48
36. Upcycled Tie Necklace _____ 49
37. Wrapped Bracelets from An Old Tee _____ 50
38. Leather Hair Tie _____ 51
39. Laced Up Collar Sleeves _____ 52
40. Bow Back T-Shirt _____ 53
41. Upcycled Sweater Slipper Boots _____ 54
42. Sweater into Skirt _____ 55
43. Tulip Skirt _____ 56
44. Summer Shorts _____ 57
45. Head Band from Old T-shirt _____ 58
46. Skirt from Discoloured T-Shirt _____ 59
47. Denim Tiffin Bag _____ 60
48. Woollen Cowl from An Old Sweater _____ 62

49. Fringe Belt	62
50. Trendy T-Shirt Bag	63
51. Braided Bracelets	66
52. Floral Print Jeans	66
53. Scarf from Striped Pyjamas	68
54. Mittens from An Old Sweater	69
Home Décor & Miscellaneous	70
55. Chair Made from Old Ties	70
56. Simple Pillow Cover from An Old Shirt	70
57. Cushion Cover from Worn Out T-shirt	71
58. Free Hand Door Mat with Old T-shirt	73
59. Floor Rug with Old Bed Sheets	74
60. Lamp Shade with Lace Camisole	75
61. Bunny Bed with Old Sweater	76
62. TV Cover from Old Bed Sheets	77
63. T-Shirt Dog Toy	78
64. T-Shirt Wall Art	78
65. Old Jeans Recycled into Ampersand Rug	79
66. T-Shirt Pom Poms	80
67. Garden Tool Bucket Caddy	81
68. Drop-Dead Denim: One Tough Pouf	82
69. Towel Bunny	84
70. Cotton Dishcloth	85
71. Neck Tie iPod Holder	85
72. Sweater Patch Blanket	87
73. Hot Handle Holder	88

74. Sweater Pillows _____ 89

75. Quick & Easy Coffee Cozy from An Upcycled Sweater _____ 90

76. Cushion from An Old T-Shirt _____ 90

77. Sweater Covered Pot _____ 91

78. Bed for Your Doggy _____ 92

79. Denim Shopping Bag _____ 93

80. Wall Decor with Old Scarf _____ 94

81. T-Shirt Apron _____ 95

82. Cloth Flowers _____ 96

83. Mail Bag _____ 97

84. Laundry Bag _____ 98

85. Coaster _____ 99

86. Cat Tent Using Old T Shirts _____ 99

87. Table Napkins _____ 100

88. Table Cloth _____ 101

89. T-Shirt Quilt _____ 102

90. Christmas Wreath _____ 103

91. Denim Pocket Wall Hanger _____ 103

Kids Clothes, Toys, & More _____ 105

92. Football for The Little Boy _____ 105

93. Baby Quilt _____ 106

94. Adult Socks into Toddler Pants _____ 106

95. Children's Hat made from Old Sweaters _____ 107

96. Baby Leg Warmers from An Old Sweater _____ 108

97. T-Shirt to A Toddler Dress _____ 109

98. Tie Onesie _____ 110

99. Kids' Art Apron from A Dishtowel	*111*
100. Superhero's Cape for Kids	*112*
Conclusion	*114*
Final Words	*116*
Disclaimer	*117*

Introduction

The opportunity of upcycling is everywhere around us, and we just need to let our imagination run free and create the unexpected from the "unexpected". With the power to create something new, you can convert an old sweater into a cushion cover, old ties into a chair seat, and change your old ugly jeans into brand new boyfriend jeans!

My 1st edition "Upcycling Crafts: 35 Fantastic Ideas That Takes Old Clothes to Modern Fashion Accessories, Home Decorations, & More!" was a huge hit and success, so I added 65 more crafts, and I'm now up to my 4nd edition.

I would like to take the opportunity to say thank you to all my fans and followers, and I hope you enjoy these new and creative upcycling crafts!

Happy Crafting,
Kitty

Clothes & Fashion Accessories

1. Turn Pants into Capris

Materials

- Ironing board and iron
- Sewing machine or sewing kit
- Measuring tape
- Chalk
- Scissors
- A pair of slim pants

Directions

1. Wear the pants you want to turn into Capri's. Make a chalk mark on the side of your left leg (where you want the bottom of your Capri's to be).

2. Use a full-length mirror to achieve the best idea of the end result. Adjust as desired until it looks right in the mirror. Also mark the other side. Take off the pants and lay them flat on your workspace.

3. Capri's have a signature hem of about 2 inches high. Decide how thick you want the hem to be and double that number. Add a half inch for the seam allowance and mark. Repeat for the other leg and make sure they are even. Cut off the legs at your chalk marks and make sure the back and front are even, and that the legs are also of the same length.

4. Turn the pants inside out and fold up half inch from each leg and pin. Continue to do this all the way around the leg and iron, removing the pins as you do so. Fold in once again at your first marks and iron all the way around.

5. Use thread and needle to sew a 1/8 inch away from the bottom of the hem, all the way around. Sew the top of the hem about 1/8" from the top and there you have it!

2. Ombre Four-Strand Head Wrap

Materials

- Shirt (preferably white, size L for men)
- Scissors
- Dye
- Buttons
- Needle and thread

Directions

1. Cut the end of your shirt into small strips of about one inch apart. Avoid cutting it all the way across. Leave a few inches where you will sew on the buttons later. Lay the head wrap on a piece of plastic or tarp. Twist the strands.

2. Get a foam brush, dye and a small bowl of water. Use the gloves that come with the kit. To create the ombre coloring, drip dye at the ends of your strands.

3. Moisten the brush and dab it on the painted section of the fabric, working your way up. Continue to dab it to the level of saturation desired.

4. Continue with this technique for the other strands. You may also use turquoise for 2 and lime green for the other two. Once you finish coloring, wrap the project in plastic and allow the dye to set for a few hours.

5. Throw it in the washer (by itself) and machine-dry it for a perfect look. To finish up, twist the strands and lay ends over the corresponding piece's end, and sew together to secure. Add buttons to cover the seams.

3. Cat Printed Jeans

Materials

- Ruler (optional)
- Pencil
- Small scissors
- Cardboard
- Small piece of cardstock (4 x 10 cm)
- White fabric marker (I used a DecoFabric one)
- Pair of jeans

Directions

1. Use a pencil to draw a cat head of your desired size (preferably 3 x 2.5 cm.) Before cutting out your cat, you may want to poke holes using the pencil to make it a lot easier. Use nail scissors to cut it out but regular scissors still work just fine.

2. Put a cardboard in one of the pant legs to help stretch out the fabric and make it easier to paint on. This will also make it easier to keep the marker from seeping to the other side.

3. Follow the edge of the stencil to draw the cathead outline on the pant leg. Use a fabric marker to do this, and go over it once again to make the cathead stand out nicely.

4. Continue drawing until you feel like you have the desired number of cats on that one side. The cats should be about 1 cm apart. You may use a ruler to make sure they are all lined up.

5. If you encounter a seam on the leg, simply shift your cardboard and draw a cat head and keep going. Do the same for the other leg, and let the jeans dry out for about 10 minutes.

6. Repeat the steps with the other side of your jeans. In order to seal the design, iron the jeans on the medium setting so as to prevent the design from fading in the wash. All done!

4. Indigo Tie-Dye Jeans

Materials

- Paint stirrer
- Gallon bottle
- Indigo tie dye kit
- 5-gallon bucket with lid
- Cheap Monday Jeans (c/o) (I used this pair)

Directions

1. Fill a 5-gallon bucket with warm tap water and set it in a ventilated room or outside.

2. Empty the indigo dye into the water and stir until dissolved, slowly emptying the thiox packets and soda ash into the water. Stir gently in one direction and cover with a lid.

3. Let it sit undisturbed for one hour. Meanwhile, prepare your denim for the tie-dye. The kit includes wood blocks and rubber bands to play with.

4. Twist one pant leg and tie each section with a rubber band.

5. Then, do the same for the other pant leg, very tightly for a really awesome tie-dye look and wet the fabric thoroughly, squeezing out the excess.

6. Push aside or scoop out the foamy layer at the top. Slowly submerge the denim for one to several minutes. Be sure to wear your gloves and avoid touching the dye with bare skin.

7. Now remove from the bucket and let it oxidize for about twenty minutes. On hitting oxygen, it will turn blue.

8. Squeeze out excess water and let it dry for a few hours.

9. Afterwards, wash it by hand with detergent and hang to dry. Then iron it to set the dye in. To clean your bucket, simply empty the dye bath down the drain.

5. Ombre Jeans with Bleach

Materials

- A pair of jeans
- Some old towels
- Disposable gloves
- Bleach
- 2 buckets (one with plain water and the other for the water bleach mixture)

Directions

1. Fill the first bucket with 4 liters of tap water. Add 2 liters of bleach. Follow package instructions. Wear your gloves and soak your jeans in the bleach. For a nice Ombre effect, allow the bottom half of your jeans to soak while the other half hangs over the edge of the bucket.

2. If you would like to tie dye, make knots in the jeans with rubber bands and through the whole jeans in the bucket. Let it sit for close to one hour and see the difference. However, if you need the bottom parts to be lighter, simply dip them back in the bleach.

3. Fill the other bucket with enough water to rinse the jeans. Add a tad of washing powder to the water and wash. Let it dry overnight.

I have included a bonus just for you…

FOR A LIMITED TIME ONLY – Get my best-selling book "DIY Crafts: The 100 Most Popular Crafts & Projects That Make Your Life Easier" absolutely FREE!

Readers who have downloaded the bonus book as well have seen the greatest changes in their crafting abilities and have expanded their repertoire of crafts – so it is *highly recommended* to get this bonus book today!

Get your free copy at:

ArtsCraftsAndMore.com/Bonus

6. Boyfriend Jeans

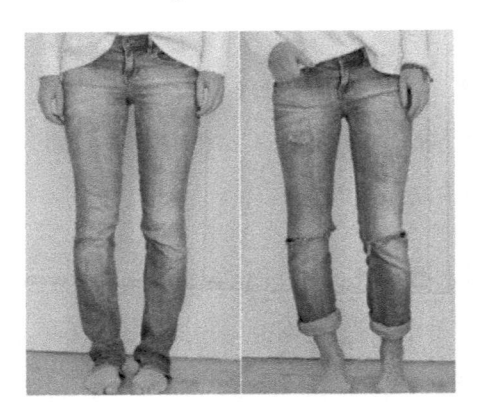

Materials

- Butter knife
- Scissors
- Boot cut jeans
- Sandpaper block
- Safety pin

Directions

1. Start off by wearing your jeans, and start cuffing the hem to ensure that when you roll the boot cut jeans, it won't get too bulky. Cuff them just above the ankle and use a safety pin to hold the cuff in place.

2. Take off the jeans (avoid cutting them while they are still on) and cut both hems at the bottom of the cuff. It's now time to distress your denim. For the big rips around the knees, begin with a small snip using your scissors. Use the butter knife to widen the hole.

3. The butter knife is great for creating frayed edges. You may also rip the hole yourself as it gets bigger. For small distressed details, just use scissors to create a couple of small slits. Take a sand paper block and rough up the holes nicely. Now roll the denim 2-3 times for the perfect boyfriend jeans. And you're done!

7. Jeans from Carrie Bradshaw

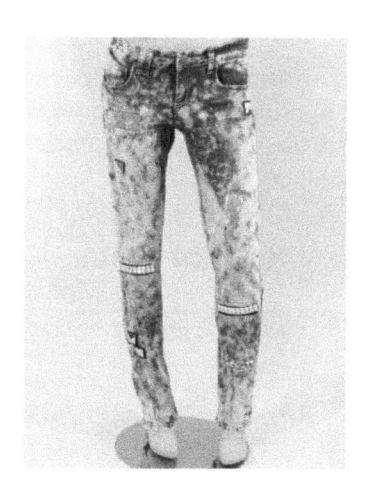

Materials

- Adhesive
- Sewing machine
- Scissors
- Pins
- Seam ripper
- Jeans- and leather-fabric and possibly felt (as an underlay)
- Studs in different sizes
- A small spoon
- Sequin fabric
- Jeans

Directions

1. Attach studs to leather pieces and cut them with about 1 cm or 0.4 inches addition. Put the small studs in rows slightly narrower than the width of the artificial leather. You should leave the fabric generously wide at the rivets. You will need to sew the rivets on the jeans so as to create the desired seam allowance.

2. Sew or glue the sequin fabric on a piece of denim fabric. Also, think of the seam allowance once more so that the rivets can be effortlessly mounted on the jeans you unstitched. Do not unstitch

the pant leg completely. It's enough to begin at about 10 cm or 4 inches above the hem.

3. Adorn the jeans with artificial leather or stud applications. Sew and fix the stud applications and sequin with pins on the inside of the jeans. Cut out the jeans so as to uncover the applications. Sew up the pant legs. Done!

8. Lace Jeans

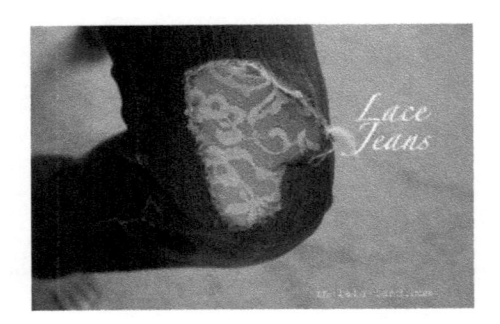

Materials

- Wood block
- Sewing thread (pick a color that closely matches your jeans)
- Needle
- Tweezers
- Tailors Chalk/ White pencil
- Lace: you only need 1/4 yard
- Old pair of your favorite jeans
- Sandpaper (optional)

Directions

1. Mark the region where you would like the lace to be on the jeans. For this case, we'll make a large patch on the left leg and another smaller patch on the right with a distressed patch on the upper right.

2. Cut out the patches nicely and cut a small slit one inch above and below the patch. Make sure the lines and the patch are of the same width. With the slits you cut, use your tweezers to pluck out loose

blue threads. There are several of them so don't give up so easily. You'll start to see the white thread, which is what we are looking for here.

3. Use the pieces you cut out of the jeans as a template for your lace. Measure out an inch from the sides and about 2 inches below and above the jeans piece and cut. Now you have the lace inserts. Turn the jeans inside out and put the woodblock between the layers. This lets you make it easier to sew down the lace and also so that you won't accidentally sew the jeans shut.

4. Lay down the lace and align it so that the best part shows through. Thread the needle and sew the lace in place. Sew about half an inch from the cut edge.

5. With the tweezers and sandpaper, start distressing the edges of jean around the lace. Pull and pluck the threads in order to expose more white. The sandpaper helps soften the jeans and lighten the dark color to give more of an aged feeling. Now pull the threads to even out the look.

9. Peplum Top

Materials

- Measuring tape
- Elastic
- Seam ripper
- Matching thread

- Zipper (optional)
- Oversized blouse (these are a dime a dozen at the thrift store)
- Sewing machine

Directions

1. Use a seam ripper to remove the sleeves from the bodice. Measure from your natural waist to your shoulder and carefully cut the blouse to that length. Set aside the extra fabric from the bottom of your blouse. This will become the peplum later on.

2. In case your material is not stretchy, you will probably have to find a zipper in the back so that you can get in and out of the shirt once it slims down. Cut a straight line at the back of your shirt for the zipper. Make the zipper go all the way down the back and leave about 3 inches at the bottom and sew the part closed. Once you finish inserting the zipper, move to the sleeves and pull the oversized sleeve up your arm. Mark with a pin how much you need to take in.

3. Also make sure the seam curves allow you some movements at the armpit. Sew with a straight seam along the dotted lines and trim off any excess fabric. Zigzag stitch and serge the raw edge to avoid fraying. Repeat the same on the other sleeve. Go back to the bodice and turn it inside out. Try it on and mark the pins where you need to take it in. Be sure to center the zipper properly. Remove the top carefully and straight sew along the marked lines. Trim off the extra fabric and once again zigzag stitch or serge the edge.

4. Attach the sleeves to the bodice. Try on the bodice and measure how wide you need the shoulder width to be. Trim the arm holes and cut them down to about 4 inches wide. With the right sides attached, pin the sleeves to the bodice.

5. Probably, the arm hole will be slightly larger than the arm hole on the sleeve. This is absolutely normal. As you pin, be sure to distribute the extra fabric evenly between the pins. Also, as you sew, stretch the fabric to avoid tucks.

6. Straight-sew around the entire sleeve and trim off the extra fabric. Zigzag stitch or serge the raw edge. After attaching the sleeves,

turn it right side out and press. As mentioned, the extra arm hole might create some waviness but it will iron out nicely as long as there are no tucks. Do the same for the other sleeve. Move the peplum and take the bottom of your blouse that you cut off and trim down if necessary so that it's completely even all the way across.

7. Take the width measurements of the bottom of the bodice and cut two pieces of the elastic (same length). Sew both ends of pieces together to form a big circle and pin it to the peplum. Sew all around the peplum, stretching the elastics as you sew. The bottom and top of the bodice should have an equal circumference measurement.

8. With the right sides attached, attach the peplum to the bodice and straight stitch. Sew next to the elastic. Be careful not to sew on the elastic! Once you finish working on the peplum, use a seam ripper to remove the elastic. Keeping it there adds bulk to the waistline—something you obviously don't want.

9. Once the elastic is removed, serge, zigzag stitch the raw edge or trim the seam allowance so as to prevent fraying. Press all the seams and you're done!

10. Lace Scarf from An Old Table Cloth & T-Shirt

Materials

- A big men's shirt
- An old lace tablecloth
- Scissors
- Sewing machine

Directions

1. Cut off the body of the t-shirt by making a straight cut across under the armpits. This leaves you with a loop of fabric hemmed on one side. Now you have an infinity scarf right there. However, it's still lacking in fabric and this is where the tablecloth comes in.

2. Cut along one of the side seams so as to turn the loop into a strip. Measure the width of the strip and cut a strip of lace that is of the same width as the loop. Measure the length depending how much lace you would like in the scarf.

3. Now pin the ends of your t-shirt strip and lace strip together to create a loop once again. Zigzag stitch the pieces together or use a serger. Hem the raw shirt/lace edge. There you have it!

11. T-Shirt Wrap Skirt

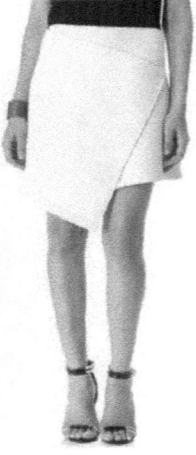

Materials

- Tape
- Thread
- Needle
- Scissors
- 2 buttons
- Old t-shirt

Directions

1. To start with, get your tape and mark a straight line across the shirt starting under the armpits. This is where you will cut the shirt.

2. Place the body of the shirt on a table, and mark the center of the skirt using tape. Now you are about to cut the skirt, so that it will no longer be a loop, but it will be a strip. From top to bottom you will make a diagonal cut to create the slanted wrap look. Now put the skirt on your waist and mark where you want to place the buttons using chalk. Also mark where you want to tie.

3. Make a strip from the unused bits of material, or use some ribbon. The next step is to place the button where you have marked on the skirt, and sew them on by hand. Once you do that, mark the skirt where the 2 parts should meet, fold your ribbon or strip of material and sew it at that spot where the 2 parts will meet. Then use the ribbon r strip and the button to secure the two parts together.

12. Cute Ruffled T-Shirt

Materials

- 2 craft t-shirts (one in your size and the other in an XL to use as pattern)
- Scissors
- Sewing machine

Directions

1. Lay out your craft shirt (your current size) over the XL shirt and trace. Try to be generous by about 1 inch. To achieve symmetry, fold over the shirt and then cut out the shape of your shirt.

2. Cut out the new neckline. To do this, you will need to fold the shirt (your size originally) in half. Sketch a line marking on your new neckline. Feel free to play around with where you would like it to fall.

3. Cut out the new neckline. Before attaching any ruffles, you first need to cut the front of your shirt in order to create a panel for attaching the ruffles. To do this measure about 3-4 inches down from the bottom of the scoop in the neckline and use a straight edge to help mark a straight line across the shirt. Cut out the panel using this marking. To make this a little clearer, the panel is where you attach ruffles. This panel should consist of the material on the front of the shirt 3-4 inches below the scoop of the neckline. After the ruffles are attached to the panel we will later reattach the panel to the shirt.

4. To make the ruffles, grab the shirt (XL shirt) and cut off the sleeves and the top of the shirt, by making a straight cut across the shirt under the armpits. Now cut 2 1/2" wide strips. Loosely ruffle each strip using a basting stitch. The strips need to be long to span the length of your panel. Pin on one ruffle at a time, sewing in place as you go. Overlap the ruffles.

5. Once you finish sewing all the ruffles (approximately 13), attach the shirt panel to the front of your shirt. Lay the top edge of the panel on the front of your tee, matching it to the edge you cut off. Pin and sew the panel back on to the shirt, so that the seam will not show.

13. T-Shirt Dress

Materials

- Sewing machine
- Pins
- Tape measure
- Scissors
- 1 T-shirt at least 2 sizes larger
- 1 t-shirt (your size but one that is a little long)

Directions

1. Lay your t-shirt (your size but long) flat on a table. Take the T-shirt that is 2 sizes long and cut the body of the shirt off. Do this by cutting a straight line across the shirt, starting under the armpits.

2. Cut open the side seams on the body piece the shirt. This will create a strip to make the skirt part of the dress.

3. Sew two parallel stitch lines along the cut edge of the skirt piece. Use a big stitch so that you'll gather easily. Pull the bobbin threads and gather the skirt.

4. Lay out the top of your t-shirt on a table and place the skirt on top (upside down and inside out). Carefully adjust the gathers so that they are even all the way around and pin.

5. Sew the skirt to your t-shirt. Use a stretch stitch on your machine; otherwise just go for a very small stitch.

14. Shirt to Dress Upcycle

Materials

- 3 old shirts
- 1/8" wide elastic
- Matching thread
- Sewing machine

Directions

1. Start off by cutting the tops off of 2 of the shirts right at the armpit. Take the top tee (the one that isn't cut up) and just slice off the hem. Attach the 2 bodies together by sewing them together, and then attach that to the bottom of the t-shirt. This should create a longer dress.

2. Take in the sides of your dress so that it's fitted well. The ruching is very forgiving so you don't have to worry too much about it becoming really tight. If it's too loose then it will sag. Finish the raw edges with a zigzagged or serged seam if desired.

3. Measure from your natural waist down to the knee and cut the elastic accordingly. Now pin one end of the elastic to the natural waist area on the side seam allowance for the dress. On the inside of the dress. Pin the other end of the elastic to the hem of the dress. Repeat the steps on the other side of your dress.

4. Now you must sew in the elastic, sew the elastic as you sew the elastic in place where you have pinned, you must stretch the elastic as you sew, if you don't it will not ruch the material, it will just be sewn into the dress.

5. The next step is optional. If you need a pocket, simply cut a piece of fabric and fold the top edge down. Sew a straight seam across. Fold the remaining sides in and press them into place and pin to the t-shirt. Sew around the tree sides. All done!

15. One Shoulder T-Shirt

Materials

- Safety pin
- T-shirt
- Scissors

Directions

1. Start this project by cutting one sleeve off your t-shirt at the seam. Now take your scissors and cut the collar or neckline out of your shirt.

2. Then put on the shirt. Measure where you would like the sleeveless part of your shirt to fall. You should begin by making a mark under the armpit. Take the shirt off and lay it flat on a table and take a pair of scissors and make a gradual diagonal cut from inside

neckline of the tank top sleeve to the mark you made under the arm. The t-shirt material will also curl over to create a nice look.

3. Now looking at your shirt you should now have a shirt with one sleeve as a tank top and the other side sleeveless with a beautiful gradual diagonal neckline. So now you have created the one shoulder shirt.

4. Now take your scissors and carefully cut the tank top strap. By making a horizontal put on the shoulder strap. Now take the scissors and make a vertical cut so the strap will now have two straps. Do this in both the bottom piece of the strap and top piece of the strap. Now take your 2-bottom piece and tie them together in a simple tie.

5. Now take the corresponding top piece and tie it to the corresponding bottom piece into a bow. You may also twist the piece before tying into a bow. Repeat this step for the 2nd set of straps. So now you have turned your single tank top strap into two straps tied with a bow.

16. Side Laced-Up DIY T-Shirt

Materials

- T-shirt
- Scissors
- Ruler
- Ribbon
- Chalk

Directions

1. Choose an old t-shirt, it could be multi-coloured or just one color. Make a cut up the side seam of the shirt up to the armpit, and repeat this on the other side seam. It's best if you use a t-shirt without sleeves. If yours has, cut the sleeves off to make a tank top. The next step is to use a ruler to measure the sides of your t-shirt.

2. Mark with chalk at every two inches along the seam you just cut. You will probably need just 2 or 3 marks on the two sides.

3. Now make the cuts. However, be careful when you do this since you don't want to end up with holes that are too big. If you like, you may add metal eyelets on each hole so as to make the shirt even better.

4. The last step involves adding the ribbon. You may use a ribbon that matches the color of your t-shirt, if you like.

5. If the t-shirt has sleeves, when cutting them off, you may cut 2 strips and then just stretch them to get one really long stripe and use that as your ribbon.

17. Bleach-Dipped Aztec Jeans

Materials

- Old Jeans
- Permanent marker
- Bleach
- Cardboard piece

Directions

1. Dip a few inches of your old jeans into watered down bleach. Leave it there for about 2-3 hours. Wash the bleach out and let them dry.

2. Once it's dry, start drawing your Aztec pattern. Place a piece of cardboard in the leg, to prevent bleeding through. You might want to sketch out your desired pattern with a pencil before drawing on them with a permanent marker.

3. Once you finish one leg, line it up with the other one and copy the pattern. Do not forget to mirror it! Do the same for the back. That's it!

18. Jeans with Patches

Materials

- Contrast color thread and needle
- Pins
- Grosgrain fabric in a stripe or other fabric you want to add
- Extra denim from another pair of jeans
- 1 Pair of old ripped jeans

Directions

1. Lay your old ripped jeans flat and measure your extra fabric and denim to make the patches. You'll need patches for the inside of your jeans where the holes are as well as more decorative patches for the outside of your jeans.

2. Pin the patches on the inside of your jeans and use the needle and thread to sew them on. You may want to use a black thread in order to make the stitches large and visible for the hand patched look.

3. Lay the jeans flat and place all the patches on your jeans. Overlap them and mix up the denim and other fabric to get the best combination. Once you finish arranging the patches, pin them to your jeans.

4. Fold all the edges of your patch where you want them and then pin them to the jeans. You may leave the raw edges if you like; it just comes down to how you want your jeans to look.

5. Again, use the needle and thread to sew the patches to your jeans. Large whipstitches look really awesome, if you prefer a more handmade look. You may choose to mix up the patches and put some horizontal and others vertical to give it a haphazard yet awesome look.

19. The Splatter-Paint Trend

Materials

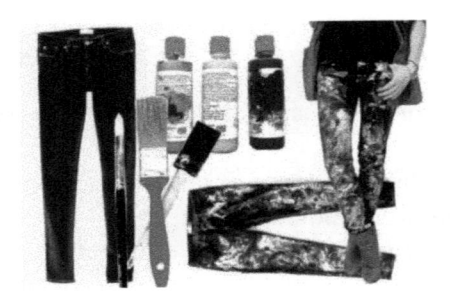

- Drop cloth or a newspaper
- Old pair of jeans (preferably the classic, skinnier cut for the best look)
- Fabric paint
- Paint brushes

Directions

1. Cover an even surface with a drop cloth or newspaper and lay your jeans down flat. Brush random strokes of the paint onto the jeans.

2. Using the paintbrush, gently flick the paint splotches and spots to blend with the strokes. Allow the jeans to dry flat before wearing. Very simple project with amazing results!

20. Sexy Cut Up Leggings

Materials

- A pair of old leggings
- Sewing machine
- Yarn and needle
- Crayon
- Pins
- Scissors

Directions

1. To start this project, you need to lay your leggings down on a flat surface. Now you will be cutting a rectangle out of the leggings just below the hip and down to mid-calf. Only on the front side of the legging though. Do this to both legs.

2. Now take that rectangle and make strips out of it long ways. About 1 ½ inch wide. Now you need to hem each side of the strips with your sewing machine.

3. Next you need to take those strips and measure them to the empty space in your leggings, and cut them to the width of the rectangle with ½ an inch on each side to sew. Next take those strips and make a crisscross pattern along the front, and sew them into place.

21. Dip Dyed Pleated Skirt

Materials

- 1 cup salt
- Dye
- 1 old pleated skirt

Directions

1. Prepare an area where you will be dying the old pleated skirt. You may use a sink, plastic container, or anything along this line. Make sure the area around the sink is clear just in case the dye splashes.

2. Fill the bucket or sink with hot tap water about halfway. Pour in the packet of dye and mix well.

3. Lay the skirt over the edge over the bucket with the end you would like to dye laying in the dye. Add 1/2 a litre more of dye and let the skirt sit in the dye bath for about three hours. The longer you leave it in the dye the better.

22. Ruffle Necktie Tee

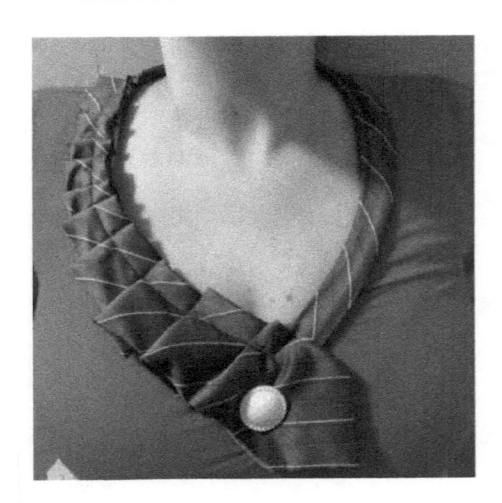

Materials

- Needle & thread
- Sewing machine
- Button

- Tie
- Old V-neck tee

Directions

1. Start the project with the small end of the tie and left side of the neckline. Lay the tie on top of the neckline and sew straight.

2. Continue sewing a straight line on the left side of the neckline as well as the back of the neckline. Stop when you get to the seam on the top right shoulder. Create ruffles by folding the tie upward and sewing on top. Continue to fold and sew to the end.

3. Once this is finished, just lay the end of the tie flat and continue sewing until you meet up with the beginning stitch on the left side. Grab your cute button and sew it right onto your shirt.

23. DIY No Knit Scarf

Materials

- A ruler
- A pair of scissors
- Leather scrap
- Super glue
- A 6oz skein of soft yarn

Directions

1. Transform the soft skein of yarn into a hank of yarn (should be loosely wound into a large ring shape and twisted).

2. To make a scarf that can be doubled up around the neck, simply set 2 heavy chairs side by side and cut a three-inch piece of yarn and reserve it for later use.

3. Now anchor your yarn to the top of a chair and wrap it tightly around the chairs (tighter wounds make better scarfs).

4. Pull the hank off the chairs carefully and twist it a few times. Lay it flat on a table. Tie together the start and end pieces around the yarn in order to keep the hank secured.

5. Tie a third section of your scarf using small pieces of yarn (the ones you cut earlier) this divides the hank into thirds. The next step is to cut three pieces of leather at about 4" long and 1.75" wide. Cover the spots you secured with yarn with the leather buts by wrapping the leather around and super gluing it closed.

24. Buttoned Up Infinity Scarf

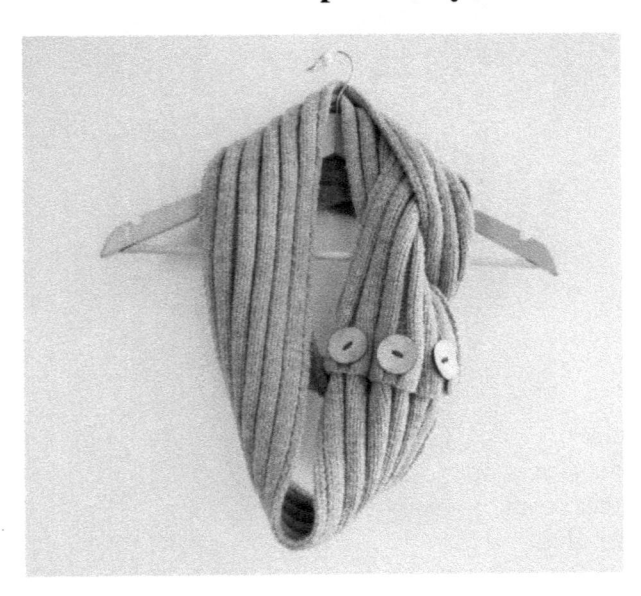

Materials

- Buttons
- Old knit scarves
- Leftover pieces of yarn

Directions

1. Cut out three pieces of yarn for the buttons. It's perfectly alright to double up on the yarn for more stability. Red colors go well with a grey scarf (just to add some warmth).

2. Take the 3 pieces of yarn and poke the yarn through the buttonholes. Use a skewer to poke the yarn through the scarf. Triple knot or just double knot those pieces of yarn.

25. Re-Styled T-Shirt with Socks

Materials

- Scissors
- Thread
- Needle
- Socks
- T-shirt

Directions

1. Cut off the heel and toe of the pair of socks. Create cuffs by folding up the end and sewing in place.

2. Now find a shirt that matches your socks, and sew them into place.

26. Woven Top

Materials

- Old worn-in top
- Grey sweatshirt

Directions

1. Lay your top flat on your workspace face down. Cut the entire back of the shirt from the base of the shirt to the top into 1 ½ to 2-inch strips.

2. Work from the seam in, measuring towards the center so as to get semi-even strips. Avoid cutting the side seam (this is where you are going to attach the fabric.)

3. Use contrasting fabric of similar stretch/weight, for example a knit mesh in cream. Use 1/4 of a yard. You may consider cutting up another old t-shirt if you need to downsize your wardrobe to make one shirt from two.

4. Cut up that fabric in 1 ½ to 2-inch strips. Weave these pieces through the pieces you have cut in the shirt and pin them into the seam. Avoid turning them since this will cause awkward bulges and bumps. You may turn the shirt inside out, particularly if you are having problems keeping things pinned and lined up.

5. Once you finish pinning everything, sew along your shoulder and side seams. Use grey thread to match your top and turn it inside out. Cut off any excess material that may create bulk.

27. T Shirt to Ruffled Dress

Materials

- Old skirt leftovers
- Elastic
- Scissors
- Needle and thread

Directions

1. Begin the upcycle project by marking your t-shirt just under the bust. Leave 4 inches under the bust and cut the rest in stripes of about 7 cm. Optional: Connect all in one long stripes to avoid fraying.

2. Now make the ruffles and pin them to the t-shirt neckline. Sew on the ruffles and sew the skirt to the bottom of the shirt.

28. Cool Summer Fringe Top

Materials

- 2 identical tops
- A sewing kit
- Pony beads
- Scissors

Directions

1. Start the project by taking one of the old tank tops. Cut it apart up the side seams. This creates a front and back piece.

2. Cut a long bib shape from the front piece you just made. Be careful though since the ending shape of the fringe top will depend on how

the initial shape turns out. Use scissors to cut the fringe vertically. Do it carefully to avoid cutting through the tops neckline.

3. The fringe bib is now complete. You should pull each fringe carefully so as to make it curl up on itself. When you tug on a standard t-shirt, it curls up nicely. Again, be careful not to pull it too much!

4. Pin the bib to the front of the other tank top. The two necklines and should line up exactly with both right sizes facing up.

5. Sew the two parts together. Use stretch or zigzag stitch. The decision to add beads or not depends on how you want your t-shirt to look.

29. Workout T-Shirt

Materials

- Old t-shirt (any color will do just fine with or without an application on it)
- Scissors

Directions

1. Cut off the ribbed neckline as well as the bottom hem. As for the sleeves, simply cut downwards and be sure to start at the

shoulders. Determine how thick you need the straps to be. Cut straight down and curve down below the armpit seam.

2. Once you finish this, decide how low you want the front neckline to be and cut away. Turn your t-shirt to the back and create a narrower racerback. Then cut a deep "V" shape from the top neckline.

3. The next thing is to stretch the bottom hemline that you just cut, until it becomes a long string of fabric. This is pretty fun to do!

4. About 2 or 3 inches above the bottom of the V shape, tie a knot and wrap a scrap strip all the way down around the center of the racerback. Now back up to meet the other ends and knot the ends together nicely, cutting off any loose ends.

5. If you need to make this a high-low top, lay the shirt sideways and flat it. Start at about 4-5 inches from the front of the shirt and cut diagonally until you reach the back. Now you have your new workout t-shirt!

30. T-Shirt Twirly Skirt

Materials

- Measure tape
- Pins
- Sewing machine
- Scissors
- Fabric
- One old t-shirt

Directions

1. Begin by cutting a straight line across the shirt under the arm pit. Make sure that you have enough fabric left over for a sash at the end. Remember this when folding it. Then measure from the corner fold out to your radius.

2. When the measurement is ready, attach your shirt to the fabric and pin them together. Sew the shirt and fabric together to form the base of your skirt.

3. In this particular craft, we are focused on making a sash. So, begin with scrap pieces of fabric. Make sure it is long enough to go all the way around the waist of the skirt and is able to tie.

4. Fold the material long ways and sew along the cut edge to form a seam with pattern side not showing. Turn the material ride side out after you have sewn it.

5. Iron and hand-stitch the opening closed afterwards. Then attach it to the dress and sew it. With this, you get the final look of this awesome dress project.

31. Tote Bag

Materials

- Scissors
- Long fabric strip (for straps)
- Dish sponge or acrylic paint
- King size pillowcase (you could also use a standard size if you want a smaller bag. Our measurements will be 41" x 21")

Directions

1. Lay your pillowcase flat so that the open end faces you. Grab the open-end side and fold it half way up.

2. Cut out your preferred shape from an ordinary dish sponge. Choose a nice pattern for your bag and use it as a stamp. Dab it in paint to create your awesome design.

3. Cut small holes on the ends of your pillowcase so as to attach the straps where the open end meets the back layer. Grab the fabric and knot it on both sides. Now weave three pieces of fabric together for a braided look.

4. Turn the bag over and bring the two bottom corners together. Attach them by cutting out a small hole in each corner and knot them together using a small piece of fabric.

5. To create a nice tassel, grab some of your scrap fabric and wrap it around the center of the flap.

32. No Sew Crop Top! (With Hemming Option)

Materials

- Scissors
- Large non-stiff tee shirt
- If hemming: thread, iron, sewing machine

Directions

Note: If hemming then you'll need to allow additional seam (Read Direction #4).

1. Cut off the sleeves. Cut the neckline and figure out how skinny you need the shoulder straps to be and cut the sleeve or necklace further in or out.

2. Cut the bottom to create a crop top.

3. Optional—hem the neckline and shoulder a half inch and bottom by 1 inch. If you're hemming then remember to add the seam allowance when cutting.

33. No-Sew Cardigan

Materials

- Scissors
- Ruler
- Old shirt
- Hem tape
- Iron
- Thread
- One button

Directions

1. Using a ruler, draw a straight line down the front center of your old shirt and cut.

2. Hem the trimmed edges using your iron and hem tape. Remember to follow the manufacturer's directions.

3. Pick your oversized button and sew it on one of the sides. It should be on the side where normal buttons theoretically go. This is what shows that your cardigan is really legit.

34. No-Sew T-Shirt Bow Sleeves

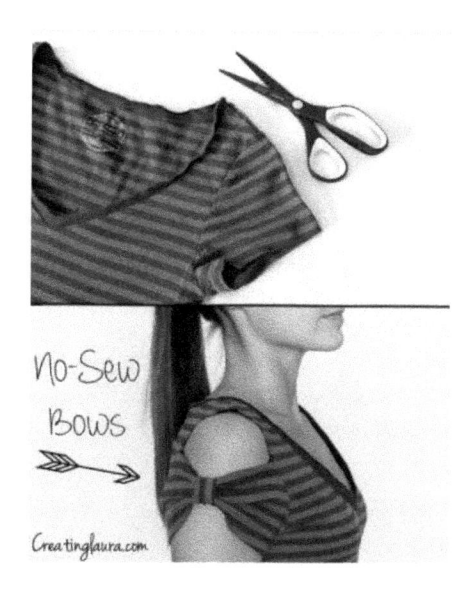

Materials

- A measuring tape
- Machine washable glue
- Scissors
- T-shirt

Directions

1. On the sleeve of your t-shirt make a 3-inch slit next to the shoulder seam. Using that slit cut out a small strip of fabric. Fold the strip in half and unfold it. Measure and cut it into two 2.5-inch strips.

2. Pinch the center of the sleeves using your fingers and wrap one of the strips around the sleeve where you pinched it. Put a dab of glue on the tip of the strip.

3. Fold the other end of the strip with glue so that it's a circular band around the sleeve. Pinch it between the fingers to secure the glue and repeat steps on the other sleeve. Allow the glue to dry before trying on your new creation.

35. Men's Shirt into A Handbag

Materials

- 2 round wooden handles
- Fabric for the bag lining and trim
- Scissors
- Ruler
- Old t-shirt
- Sewing machine

Directions

1. Cut a rectangle from the center of the old t-shirt (preferably 16.5" x 12.5" or 42 x 34cm) through both layers. The size of your rectangle should reflect the desired size of your bag.

2. For both the outer and inner bag fabric, pin the rectangle right sides together along the three sides, leaving the top opening of the bag. Flatten the corners and put your hand inside the pocket so as to box the corners out.

3. Stitch along the corners about 5cm (2") in from the tip and cut off the points beyond the stitching. Repeat this for the bottom corners and gather the tops of both pieces by running a line of stitching around the top of each piece about 5cm (2") in from the top.

4. Make sure the stitches are on the longest setting. To do this, stitch two separate lines on either side of your bag. Pull the threads at the ends to "gather" the tops of the pieces of the bag (sort of closing a drawstring bag).

5. Make sure the inner bag has the right sides facing inwards and the outer bag has the right sides out. Insert the inside of the bag in the outer bag. Pin both sides together along the stitch line.

6. To make the top rim of your bag, fold the top of the outer bag over and fold the inner fabric in the same way, tucking the raw edge just below the line of stitching. Do this all round the top of the bag, pinning it into place. Top stitch the bag all the way round.

7. To make the handles, cut two rectangles of the inner fabric (preferably 15 x 8cm (6 x 3")) and double fold the short edges over and stitch. Wrap one of the rectangles around, tucking raw edges in to make the handle. Pin together and stitch along the pinned handles. Decorate it with simple yoyo fabric and a button in the center.

36. Upcycled Tie Necklace

Materials

- Tie
- Beads
- Scissors

Directions

1. Begin by deconstructing the tie, starting from the back. Carefully split the stitches and remove the guts. Do this carefully to avoid tearing or putting a hole in the tie. Iron Flat.

2. Trim the tie into a long strip from one end to the other. Note that this will vary from tie to tie and skinny ties won't work well unless you have smaller beads.

3. Fold the trimmed tie in half right sides together and sew to close the bottom end. Continue all around and stop after about 3 inches and back stitch. Skip 2 inches and start again.

4. Turn the tie right side out through the opening and press flat. Tie a knot at every 7 inches and insert a bead. Repeat this for about 8 times and leave about 7 inches of space for the bow and an option to lengthen or shorten your necklace. Hand-sew the hole sealed.

37. Wrapped Bracelets from An Old Tee

Materials

- Old T-shirts
- A bunch of bangle bracelets

Directions

1. Cut your old t-shirt in ½ to 1-inch wide strips. Depending on the thickness of your bangles—thick bracelets will require thicker strips.

2. Take one strip of the t-shirt strip and tie one end to the bangle and wrap fabric around the bracelets—the tighter the better.

3. Wrap the strips around the bracelet all the way to the first knot. Untie the knot and tie both ends together to close. Make a tight double knot and make sure the knot is positioned on the inside of your bracelets. Alternatively, you may use a glue gun to secure the ends. Using a pair of scissors, trim the ends carefully.

38. Leather Hair Tie

Materials

- Leather
- Scissors
- A ruler
- Hair bands
- Twist ties

Directions

1. Measure a strip of leather that's 1/2 inch in width and 15 inches in length and cut. Make sure the piece is as even as possible. Trim both ends of the strip so that they come to a gradual point.

2. Place the strip of leather on top of your hair band and use a twist tie to secure them together. Make sure the leather is properly lined up so as to get two equal lengths. Put hair in a ponytail and make sure the twist tie used is secured at the top. This is because it will eventually be covered up by the knot.

3. Wrap both ends of your leather strips in opposite directions, under your ponytail to cover up the hair band. Tie them in a double knot just above the twist tie so that it's secure.

39. Laced Up Collar Sleeves

Materials

- Old t-shirt
- Leather string
- Sewing machine
- Eyelet Grommet Pliers Set or metal grommet trimming

Directions

1. Take a pair of scissors and cut along the seam from the end of the sleeve to the neck hole. Repeat on other sleeve.

2. Add eyelets to each side of the slit, and weave the leather string through the eyelets.

40. Bow Back T-Shirt

Materials

- An old t-shirt, a scoop or crew neck will work just fine
- Scissors
- Seam ripper (optional)
- Thread and needle or a sewing machine

Directions

1. Make light markings on the back of your old t-shirt for how wide you want the cut-out to be and how far down the old t-shirt you want to go. Cut out a "U" shape in the back upward from the bottom hemline. Do it carefully to avoid cutting through both sides!

2. Cut out the pieces for the bow they should be about 1 inch tall. You should have 2 of these rectangle sections cut out. Evenly spaced on the back of the shirt.

3. Create a bow using the cut fabric by wrapping it around the back cut-outs. Secure the bow in place by sewing the fabric around the bows.

41. Upcycled Sweater Slipper Boots

Materials

- Scissors
- Yarn
- Pins
- Old sweater (preferably one with a tight enough weave so that it doesn't unravel when you cut it)
- Tape measure
- A large darning needle

Directions

1. Trace your foot by making a rough outline of foot on cardstock or sheet of paper. Allow about 1 ½ cm of extra space around the edges for easy sewing and comfy slippers. Cut out the shape and repeat with the other foot.

2. Cut the sole pieces and place the cutouts on the body area of the sweater. Cut around them so as to create two sole pieces. It's advisable to use a double-sided tape to prevent the paper from slipping as you cut. Measure for the leg part of your slipper boots, by trying on the sweater arms on your legs since these will serve as the boot part.

3. Snip the region around the foot carefully, cutting the fabric of the sleeve away from the sole of your foot. Ideally, this is to avoid your foot from being exposed. Repeat the same for the other foot.

4. Pin it together and connect the pieces to the other leg piece using large pins. Begin with one pin at the toe of your boot and another at the heel. Now stretch the fabric so that the two pieces line up and pin them together.

5. With the large pins in place, blanket stitch the leg piece and sole piece together. Push the needle through the two layers of fabric from the top. Pull the yarn through until a small loop remains and bring the needle back down through the loop and pull to tighten the yarn.

42. Sweater into Skirt

Materials

- Pins
- Scissors
- Wide elastic (the width of your waist)
- Sweater 1 or 2 sizes bigger than your usual size (Note that the waist of the sweater should fit your hips)
- Sewing machine

Directions

1. Cut off the top of the sweater, by cutting a straight line across the sweater underneath the armpits.

2. After removing the top of the shirt, hem this cut edge. Take the other end of the skirt, and this will serve as the top of the skirt.

3. Slightly stretch out the elastic as you pin it into the waist of the skirt, and sew in place with a zigzag stitch.

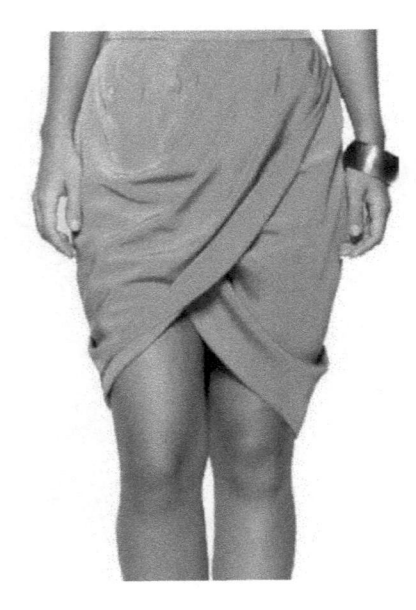

43. Tulip Skirt

Materials

- Old skirt
- Sewing machine
- Scissors
- Tailor's chalk
- inch Elastic (enough to wrap around your waist)
- Matching thread
- At least 2 yards of knit fabric (depending on your measurements)

Directions

1. To start off making your tulip shaped skirt you need to take your fabric and cut a piece measuring 36 inches in height and width measured to your waist with a few inches to sew seams.

2. Fold the fabric in half width ways, while making a mark with your chalk about 15 inches from the top along the cut edge.

3. Now you need to make marks where you will cut this piece of material. Starting at the 15-inch mark you made, make a curved line to the top of the folded edge, and starting again at the 15inch mark make a curved line down to the bottom corner of the folded edge.

4. Cut along the marks you have just made while the fabric is still folded. Now baste stitch 2 rows at the top of your skirt while, and make sure to gather your fabric evenly.

5. Take your elastic and measure it to your waist, but cut it 1 inch shorter than your waist measurement, and pin the elastic into the top of your skirt. Using a zigzag stitch sew in the elastic at the top of your skirt. Make sure to stretch the elastic as you sew it in.

44. Summer Shorts

Materials

- Sewing machine or serger
- Old leggings
- Pins
- Scissors

Directions

1. Put on your old pair old leggings and measure to the point you would like your shorts to start. Take of the leggings and fold them in half as to copy the mark you just made on one leg onto the other leg, to make the marks even.

2. Take your scissors, and make a cut across the leggings one inch below the mark you just made. Turn the leggings inside out and fold up the bottom as to form a hem and pin. Using a zigzag stitch to sew the hem.

45. Head Band from Old T-shirt

Materials

- Old t-shirt
- Sewing machine
- Scissors
- Measuring tape

Directions

1. Take your old t-shirt and lay it on a flat surface. Cut off the top of the shirt by making a cut under the armpit across to the other armpit, and discard this piece.

2. Cut up the side of the body near the seam to make a large piece of fabric, and fold this fabric in half.

3. Now take a measurement of your head, for where your headband would sit. Make a mark on your fabric along the longest cut edge of the fabric with this measure plus 1-½ inches for a seam.

4. Now take your measuring tape and make a 6-inch mark along the shorter cut edge of the fabric plus 1-½ inches for a seam. Cut the fabric to these measurements, and pin the fabric.

5. Sew the fabric along the edge, and when you have 2 inches left, turn the fabric right side out and hand stitch the rest of the headband.

46. Skirt from Discoloured T-Shirt

Materials

- Discoloured t-shirt
- Fabric paint and brush
- Sewing machine
- Elastic tape
- Scissors and fabric marker

Directions

1. All measurements are subject Cut off the sleeves and neck parts of the t-shirt. Keep the hem so that you do not have to make it again.

2. Cut the cloth in 2 halves. One will be a rectangle and will make the upper part of the skirt and the other will be long and wide strip, to make the frills at the bottom.

3. Paint the pieces (stripes will look great) to hide the discoloured parts.

4. Take the long strip and gather it together and sew in a seam to make the frills.

5. Fix the elastic tape at the waist and iron the skirt from the opposite side. Take the frills and sew them to the bottom section of the skirt. Making sure that you sew it inside out to hide the seams.

47. Denim Tiffin Bag

Materials

- Worn out denim pants
- An old belt
- Strong transparent thread
- Scissors
- Sewing machine
- Thick needle for hand stitching

Directions

1. Cut one leg of the denim pant to make the body of the bag. Stitch the upper end with the sewing machine from the inside. Sew the seam inside out to hide the seam, and when finished return to normal.

2. Take the belt and sew the buckle at the middle of the bag, but not with the flap.

3. Now, wrap the belt vertically around the bag and sew it to the top part of the flap. The buckle will be used to close the bag as you will just have to draw the belt end through the buckle and lock into place.

48. Woollen Cowl from An Old Sweater

Materials

- Old sweater
- Cloth strips
- Needle and thread
- Scissors

Directions

1. Make a cut under the arms of the sweater and straight across. This creates the cowl shape. Sew the cotton strips along the edges, as a binding to prevent the yarn strands from fraying and unravelling.

49. Fringe Belt

Materials

- Old cotton shirt
- Scissors
- Velcro
- Flower motif and hot glue

Directions

1. Cut the sleeves and collar off of your shirt, by making a cut straight across the shirt starting underneath the armpits.

2. Now make a cut up one of the side seams. Now you will have a large rectangular piece. Now take this piece and measure your waist, and cut accordingly, and fix your Velcro on the opening. Now starting at the bottom cut slits up the fabric to create a fringe.

50. Trendy T-Shirt Bag

Materials

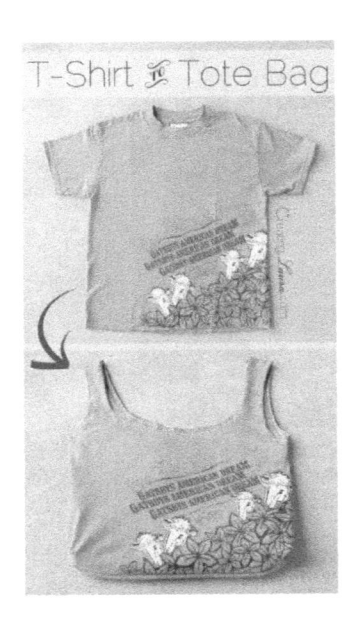

- Old t-shirt
- Pair of scissors
- Acrylic fabric paint and brush
- Needle and matching thread
- Marker pen
- Cutting board and board pins

Directions

1. Stretch the cloth on the cutting board and fix the corners tight with board pins.

2. Draw the pattern of a bag along with the handles onto the material. Make sure to make the handle parts wide enough so that they remain strong.

3. Hand stitch along the border and cut off the unnecessary parts. Now, decorate the front and back with the fabric paint and allow it to dry.

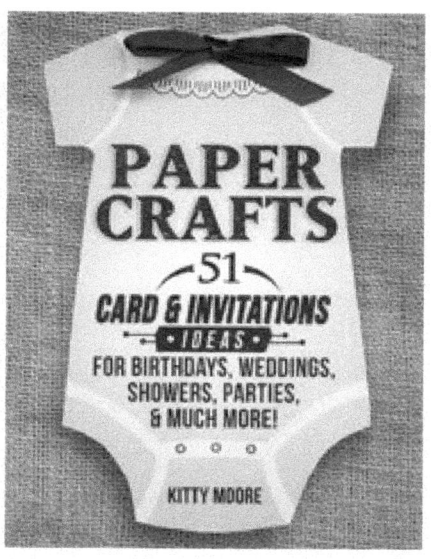

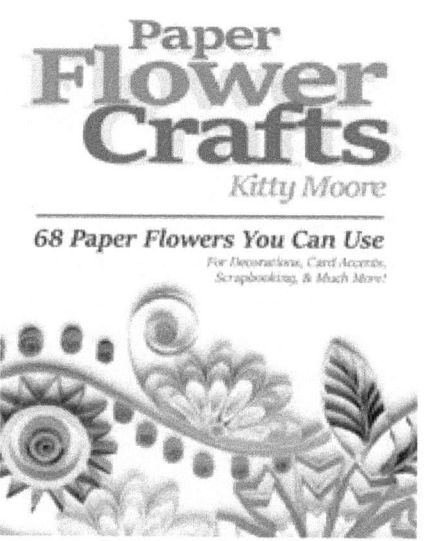

Check out Kitty's books at:

ArtsCraftsAndMore.com/go/books

51. Braided Bracelets

Materials

- Old T-shirt
- Needle and thread
- Scissors

Directions

1. Cut your t-shirt into long and narrow strips. Take 3 strips and make a braid.

2. Make the braid long enough to fit your wrist. Join the ends to make a ring and tie it tightly together.

52. Floral Print Jeans

Materials

- Cardboard
- Floral pattern or lace to trace
- Fabric markers
- White old jeans

Directions

1. Start the project at the ankle of your old jeans. If you are particularly shaky then begin at the back of the ankle. This way, if you mess up at first, chances of anyone noticing are slightly minimal.

2. Now slip a piece of cardboard between the legs, so that the marker does not transfer to the other side of the fabric. Use a lace pattern. It's ideal due to its rough, textured look it creates. Lace has a flower design which you may want to use over the entire leg for continuity.

3. Hold the lace taught and mark right through the lace onto the jeans. Bear in mind that the flowers do not have to be perfect. Repeat the same flower pattern to cover the front and back of the jeans and be sure to space the design out and tilt the flower in a variety of positions for a more free-flowing look.

4. Additionally, do not forget to place some over the seams and edges of your jeans. Seams never line up perfectly on legs.

5. You can also free hand the design if you like, particularly in between the flower patterns. Also, you may want to use a different part of the lace to create a leaf design. Add dimension with different shades of blue. Go over and around some of the edges with a darker blue for more texture and depth.

53. Scarf from Striped Pyjamas

Materials

- Old striped pyjama
- Scissors
- Rotary cutter
- Needle and thread

Directions

1. Cut the pyjamas along the length, cut off the hem part too. Make it 8" wide. Join the 2 ends by stitching.

2. On one edge of the pyjamas, make vertical cuts half way into the material to make a fringe like appearance.

54. Mittens from An Old Sweater

Materials

- Old sweater
- Scissors
- Yarn needle and matching yarn

Directions

1. Cut the sweater into the shape of mittens. Make sure you make 2 cut outs with an inch to spare around the outside of the cut out (make sure you shape the thumb correctly for both hands).

2. Sew the pieces together by hand by sewing a simple stitch around the outside of the cut-outs. Leave the hand hole open. Make a hem at the wrist part.

Home Décor & Miscellaneous

55. Chair Made from Old Ties

Materials

- Several old ties
- Wooden frame of a chair

Directions

1. To start off with take your ties and tie them on one side of the frame where you sit, and stretch them across the chair and tie on the other side.

2. Then take another group of ties and tie them on the back part of the sitting part of the chair, and weave them up through the ties that are already on the chair, and secure them with a knot on the front part of the frame.

56. Simple Pillow Cover from An Old Shirt

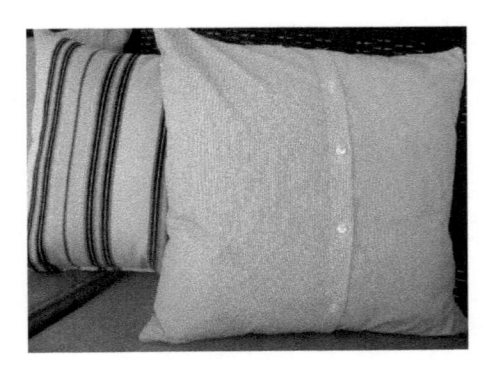

Materials

- Old men's dress shirt or a shirt with buttons
- Sewing machine
- Scissors
- Matching threads
- Flower motif (optional)

Directions

1. Take your old shirt and cut off the sleeves and collar with the scissors, by making a cut straight across the shirt under the armpits.

2. Place a square pillow on the shirt and mark the shirt where you will cut to make the pillow cover. Make sure to give yourself another 1 ½ inches extra for your seam.

3. Keep the buttons closed so that you do not have to stitch the front (this will make the buttoned opening for the pillow cover). Turn the shirt inside-out so that you can sew easily.

4. Sew the four sides and then turn the fabric right side out through the buttoned opening. Sew the flower motif to one corner. This will be the decoration for the pillow cover (this is optional).

57. Cushion Cover from Worn Out T-shirt

Materials

- Old t-shirts
- Sewing machine
- Matching threads
- Acrylic paints of a dark shade
- Fabric paint medium
- Paint brush
- Rolling cutter
- Pair of scissors
- Cutting mattress
- Pins
- Flower motif (optional)
- Wooden buttons

Directions

1. Take the measurement of the cushions and mark the T-shirts accordingly. It will be better to stretch the shirts on the cutting mattress and fix them with pins. This will ensure straight cuts. Cut off the sleeves and neck portion to make the work easy.

2. As the sides of the T-shirt are already stitched together, you will just have to sew the lower part. Leave the upper part unstitched as you will have to leave that part open to allow the cushion to be removed. Make sure that you fold the cloth inside-out before sewing. Once done, bring it back to the original position.

3. Now, you will have to make a hem at the upper end. Just fold the brim (about ½ inch) and sew it manually as the hem. You will have to use the scissors to cut the button holes here and then stitch the buttons in the right places.

4. Now, you will just need to mix the fabric medium with the acrylic paint and use your brush to draw your favorite pattern onto the pillowcase. It will be best to use a darker shade of paint as that will help to hide the faded color of the T-shirt.

5. Now, you just have to wait until the paint dries. Once the paint is dry, sew the flower motif to the corner. You can also use hot glue to fix the motif (optional). Before you put the cushion in, it is

suggested to use a hot iron to press the cloth. Make sure that you place a newspaper on the fabric paint before using the iron. This will make the cloth smooth and also fix the fabric paint to the cloth.

58. Free Hand Door Mat with Old T-shirt

Materials

- Old t-shirts (amount depends on how big you want your rug)
- Transparent thread
- Strong needle
- Pair of scissors

Directions

1. You will start by cutting the t-shirt into several strips. Convert the whole shirt into long and thin strands of fabrics.

2. Then start by making braids with the long strands. Tie both ends of the braid with thread, so that they do not open up.

3. Now start by trying the braid ends together to make one long braid.

4. Then start curling the braids onto itself to make a patty shape.

5. You will continue to join the braids, and string the thread around the rolls to hold the rug into its patty shape. Tie off the thread and there you have it!

59. Floor Rug with Old Bed Sheets

Materials

- Old bed sheets
- Transparent thread
- Thick and strong needle
- Pair of scissors

Directions

1. Start this project by cutting the bed sheets into long strips. As the sheets are rectangular in shape, it will be best to cut them along the length. You will be able to get longer strips for making the braids.

2. Take three strips and braid them together. You will have to make several braids and remember to tie both ends with thread.

3. Wrap the braids in circles and sew each layer with the previous one as you proceed. This will ensure that all the layers stay in place and the rug is strong.

60. Lamp Shade with Lace Camisole

Materials

- Pair of scissors
- Sewing needle
- Matching thread
- Hot glue
- Measuring tape
- Washable fabric marker
- Lace camisole
- Old lamp

Directions

1. Start by cutting the collar and straps off the shirt, start by making a cut straight across the shirt starting under the armpit. Measure the circumference of your lampshade. Mark this measurement on the lace. If there is some excess of the cloth, cut it off.

2. Sew the two ends of the lace to form a cylinder. Make it slightly smaller than the lampshade. This will ensure that the lace will fit snugly onto the shade.

3. Put the lace cylinder over the lamp shed and mount it as if you were putting a case on a pillow.

4. Fix the upper and lower ends with the help of hot glue. If you do not want to fix it permanently, use cold glue.

5. In case you find that the lace part is not tight on the lamp shed. Remove it and sew it once again to make the cylinder smaller than before. This will make it fit tightly.

61. Bunny Bed with Old Sweater

Materials

- Old sweater
- Yarn needle
- Matching yarn
- Synthetic filler to make the bed soft
- Washable fabric marker
- Pair of scissors

Directions

1. You will have to cut off the sleeves and neck portion of the sweater. Start by cutting straight across the sweater starting underneath the armpit. This will provide you with a loop of woollen fabric.

2. Sew the lower portion of the sweater with yarn. Fill the cylinder with synthetic filler. This will make the bed soft and comfortable.

3. Sew the upper portion of the sweater shut, so that the fillers do not come out.

62. TV Cover from Old Bed Sheets

Materials

- Old bed sheet
- Satin ribbon
- Scissors
- Sewing machine

Directions

1. Cut the bed sheet according to the size of your TV. Measure the length of your TV, and add 4 feet to the measurement.

2. Fold your ribbon in half and cut it, sew the ribbon to the bed sheet. This will allow you to tie the bed sheet to TV.

63. T-Shirt Dog Toy

Materials

- Old t-shirt
- Scissors

Directions

1. Cut 2 to 3-inch-wide slits at the base of your old t-shirts. After you've cut the slits, simply rip along the slit to form ripped strips of fabric.

2. Gather the t-shirt strips and tie off one end, dividing the strips into thirds. Braid them together. Once you've braided down to the other end, tie up the bottom. Cut any straggling t-shirt strips. This is a great gift for four-legged friend!

64. T-Shirt Wall Art

Materials

- 4 large t-shirts
- Hot glue gun
- 4 pictures frames (whatever size or shape you like)

Directions

1. Start by cutting the sleeves and collar off your t-shirts. Do this by making a cut straight across the shirt starting under the armpits.

2. Next lay your photo frames on top of each t-shirt. Hot glue the t-shirts around the photo frames.

65. Old Jeans Recycled into Ampersand Rug

Materials

- Scissors
- Lots of small t-shirt scraps
- XL t-shirt

Directions

1. Start by making the base of the rug. Lay down the XL t-shirt flat and cut a large rectangle out of the t-shirt. You may also cut the XL t-shirt into a circle shape for a regular rug. Make the scraps. Go for 10-12 t-shirts and select complimentary colors.

2. Cut the t-shirts into thin strips of about 1-1 ½ inches wide and 5-6' inches long. You may use scissors or a board and rotary cutter to help you make things faster. Don't be afraid to use imperfect scraps. They add to the nice shaggy look of your rug.

3. Cut holes into the base, starting at 1 inch from the edge, carefully poke or snip vertical and horizontal rows of small holes about 1/2 to 2/3 inches apart. If you need perfectly looking rows, you can mark the holes first using a ruler.

4. Begin at one corner and thread a strip down through the first hole and back up through the second. Thread the second scrap through the second hole so that it shares the hole with the first scrap. Pull it through the third hole.

5. This might take a while but continue until you are finished! Once you finish, give the rug a little haircut to even out longer scraps. You may leave the rug uneven for a really nice shaggier look.

66. T-Shirt Pom Poms

Materials

- Cardboard
- Scissors
- T-shirts, 1 per Pom pom

Directions

1. Use a round object to trace circles onto cardboard to make templates. Play around with the different template sizes for

different sized pom poms. Cut the shirt into half inch strips from the arm pits down and take one strip and one template.

2. Sandwich the strips by placing the other template on top. Take the fabric strips and place them on cardboard with the end even with the outer edge.

3. Wind around the templates and pull the strip tightly so that it stretches the material. Take another strip (when close to the end of the strip) and place the edge even with the outer circle like before. When winding, be sure to overlap the end of the previous strip so that it's held in place nicely.

4. Continue winding the strips around the template until you get to the other side. Do two more layers of strips. Pull the sandwiched strip tight and wrap around each other to help hold things in place for the next step.

5. Use one hand to hold the strips in place and use scissors to cut the strips along the template. Remove the template and give it a nice haircut! Sandwich the ball and cut around to make a nice round pomp. Remove the circles, fluff and trim as desired.

67. Garden Tool Bucket Caddy

Materials

- Scissors
- Thread
- Needle
- Old jeans

Directions

1. Cut around the pockets on the back of your jeans. If you need all the four pockets, you need 2 pairs. Cut out the waistline where the belt loops are and a long piece of the leg inseam with about three inches of fabric off each side of the seam.

2. Pin the pieces around the bucket and place the inseam piece around the lip of the bucket with the three inches fabric hanging around the inside and outside. Fasten the inseam using pins to hold it in place and pin the back pockets around the outside.

3. Pin the belt loops along the inside but be conscious of leaving some space to lift the bucket by the handle. Sew loops and pockets into place. You may use heavy thread or a zigzag stitch to ensure the seams are durable. Also, be sure that everything hangs out right on the bucket and then sew the inside of the inseam to itself so that the strip of pockets is a loop.

4. Add your tools and use the jeans to secure the ends of the inseam, sewing into place. Add your seeds, tools etc. and machine wash when needed.

68. Drop-Dead Denim: One Tough Pouf

Materials

- Stuffing
- Straight pins
- Sewing machine
- Pair of scissors
- Paper templates
- 5-inch round template
- 18-inch round template
- Denim scraps in different shades
- Thread, needle, Pencil, and Ruler
- Optional: dimensional fabric paint and embroidery thread

Directions

1. Using an 18-inch circle template, draw out a circle on a large piece of paper. Locate the center of the circle and figure out how big a 1/12th wedge of the circle is. The angle of the resulting wedge should measure 360°/12 = 30°.

2. Divide the wedge into 2 sections and cut off about an inch of the uppermost apex of the wedge. Draw out the individual resulting shapes on a separate piece of paper. Add ¼ inch seam allowance to the sides of each shape and cut out the pieces. These should be your pouf templates.

3. Pick one 30° wedge and add a 10inch long rectangle to its bottom. Divide the wedge from the bottom rectangle using a straight line. For each pouf template, cut out 4 each, 3 different shades of denim.

4. Get ready to sew. Pin the top wedge pieces right sides together and mix shades of denim as you go. Ensure the edges of the wedge pieces line up well. Intersect them and sew the pieces together, allowing a 1/4-inch seam.

5. Check whether the edges of the 2 pieces match after unfolding the wedge at the seam. Sew the wedge to the rectangle right sides together with a 1/4-inch allowance.

69. Towel Bunny

Materials

- Wash Cloth
- Synthetic fillers
- Sewing machine
- Plastic eyes
- Ribbon
- Small pom pom

Directions

1. Lay out a wash cloth, and in the center lay synthetic filler. Grab the corners of the washcloth and bring them together and twist right above the filler one time. Tie a strand of ribbon around the twisted area. This will serve as the body of the bunny.

2. Now take a smaller chunk of filler and place it inside the washcloth in front of the spot you just twisted. Again twist the cloth in front of the filler you just added. And tie a ribbon around it. Make sure the two showing corners are facing toward the ceiling. These are the bunny's ears. Now glue a nose and eyes to the face of the rabbit.

70. Cotton Dishcloth

Materials

- Cotton bed sheet
- Satin ribbon
- Sewing machine

Directions

1. Cut the bed sheet in squares (8"x8").

2. Sew the hem, and sew on the ribbon around the outside of the squares to make a border.

71. Neck Tie iPod Holder

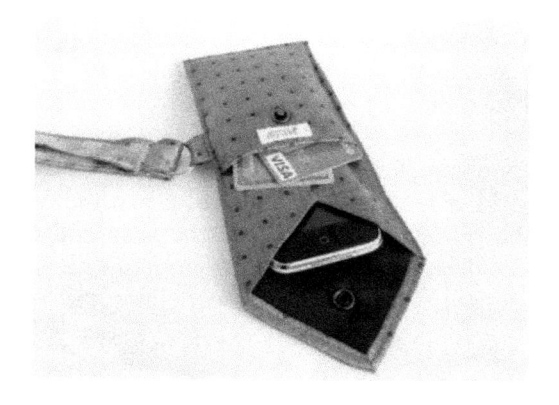

Materials

- 1 necktie
- Snap fastening pliers or snap fastener
- Decorative snap buttons
- Thread and needle
- Cutting mat
- Ruler / straight edge
- Sharp fabric scissors or rotary cutter

Directions

1. Fold the pointed end of your old tie over. Measure this from the folded edge that creates.

2. Use a sharpie to mark at 1/2 and 6 inches (perfect size for your iPhone).

3. For a different device, get their measurements by sliding it inside the end of the tie, folding the flap as if you were closing the pouch. Remember to leave room for the seam towards the bottom, about 1/2 inch. Mark for cutting.

4. Use a pair of scissors and a ruler to create a perfect straight cut. Turn the cut piece inside out and leave the lining of the tie in place so you don't have to re-stitch the seam.

5. Stitch a straight line along the end of the pouch, about half inch from the end of the fabric.

6. Fold the corners in and sew them down so as to create rounded corners for your pouch. Trim excess fabric using a pair of scissors and ruler then turn the pouch right-side out again.

7. Use a Dritz snap fastening pliers and a faux pearl snap to secure the snaps in place about 1/4 inches down the V of the opening. Repeat the process for the top of the snap and rotate the bottom part of the jaw on the snap-fastening pliers. Remember to add rubber rings to the snap fastener jaws (if included but not attached.)

72. Sweater Patch Blanket

Materials

- Sweaters
- Scissors
- Over locker

Directions

1. Start by cutting the sweaters along the sleeve seams and also along one side seam.

2. Cut as many large squares from the sweater as possible, including some seam lines and button up detail in some of the squares.

3. Cut smaller squares if you are unable to cut anymore large squares from the sweater.

4. You may use an over locker to sew the squares together and finish off all the raw edges of the cut knits.

5. Roll and blanket-stitch the entire hem. Some knits get thick and may not roll up really well so you want to go around once more and slip-stitch to keep them tightly secured. All done!

73. Hot Handle Holder

Materials

- Insul-Bright batting
- Scrap double fold bias tape
- Scrap fabric for the lining
- Old pair of jeans or old fabric

Directions

1. Cut 2 pieces of lining, 2 pieces of Insul-Bright and 2 pieces of fabric from your jeans. The material for the hot handle holder should be as wide and as long as the pot handle you would like to cover. Along with an inch for a seam.

2. Sandwich the Insul-Bright between the lining and the jean fabric. Repeat for other side of the pot hand holder. (Insul-Bright—the shiny side to the back of the jean fabric.)

3. Pin each fabric "sandwich" together to avoid shifting while you sew on the bias tape. Cut the bias tape just a bit longer than the edge of the pan holders.

4. Enfold the edge in bias tape and sew. This will be pretty thick which means you should make the stitch length longer. Now pin the 2 pieces together, main fabric back to back and sew along the outside curve. While doing this, avoid sewing the bias tape covered opening together!

5. Sew along the outside of the stitch line with a zigzag stitch and trim the edges. Turn it inside out and you are finished. For an even fancier holder, quilt the layers together before adding the bias tape.

74. Sweater Pillows

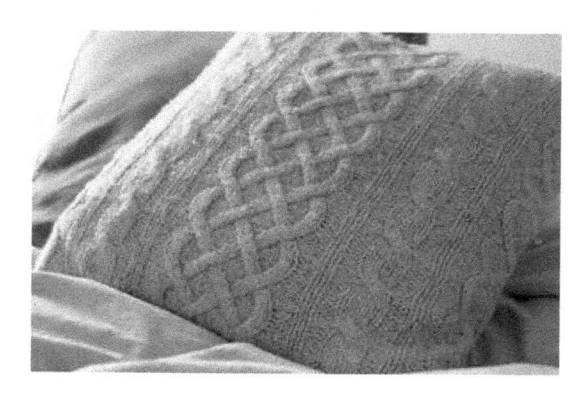

Materials

- Sweater
- Embellishments (like buttons) – optional
- Straight pins
- Sewing machine
- Needle/thread
- Scissors
- Measuring tape
- Pillow foam

Directions

1. Wash and dry your sweater. Turn it inside out. Start by making a cut straight across the sweater starting under the armpits. Then hem his cut edge.

2. Next fill the sweater with pillow foam. Next sew the opening closed. You may add any embellishments or buttons to the pillows for decorations.

75. Quick & Easy Coffee Cozy from An Upcycled Sweater

Materials

- Thread and needle (you may use embroidery thread)
- Sleeve
- Coffee cup (preferably a reusable one)

Directions

1. Start off by selecting the sweater and section you'd like to use. Cut a strip from the sweater (width of your preference) or according to your template.

2. Determine the point where the ends meet, and pin them together to secure. Flip it inside out, and stitch the two ends together. Trim the thread ends and fabric, if necessary.

76. Cushion from An Old T-Shirt

Materials

- Sewing machine
- Scissors
- Old T-shirt
- Old seat cushion

Directions

1. Cut the collar and sleeves off your t-shirt, by making a cut straight cross your shirt starting underneath the armpits.

2. Next, make sure your shirt is inside out, and hem across this cut opening.

3. Now slide your old seat cushion from the other opening, and hem across. You may add embellishments to the cushion if you wish.

77. Sweater Covered Pot

Materials

- A plant pot
- Ruler
- Scissors
- Old sweater

- Hot glue (optional)

Directions

1. Using a ruler, measure the height of your plant pot.

2. Use the measurement to cut off part of your sleeve on the old sweater. If the sweater has bands or some nice stripes that you may want to include in what you cut off so that they are part of the design. Just make sure you measure the length of the pot, and take that into consideration if you want to use something other than a sleeve in the sweater.

3. Pull the sweater piece over the pot. Fold the top of the sweater over the brim of the pot, and fill the pot with marbles or little rocks to hold the raw edge. Rocks also give a really nice finished look. The bottom tucks nicely under and stays put though you can still use hot glue to hold it down.

78. Bed for Your Doggy

Materials

- Old sweater
- Yarn needle
- Matching yarn
- Synthetic filler to make the bed soft

- Washable fabric marker
- Pair of scissors

Directions

1. You will have to cut off the sleeves and neck portion of the sweater. Start by cutting straight across the sweater starting underneath the armpit. This will provide you with a loop of woolen fabric.

2. Sew the lower portion of the sweater with yarn.

3. Fill the cylinder with synthetic filler. This will make the bed soft and comfortable. Sew the upper portion of the sweater shut, so that the fillers do not come out.

79. Denim Shopping Bag

Materials

- Old denim skirt
- Sewing machine
- Strong transparent thread
- Hot glue
- Pair of scissors
- Old Scrap
- Ribbon

Directions

1. Take the bottom hem of your skirt and sew it shut.

2. Take your ribbon and measure how long you would like your purse to hang on your shoulder. Sew both ends of the ribbon to each side of the purse.

3. Next take the scrap ribbon and string it through the belt loops on the skirt. You have finished your purse!

80. Wall Decor with Old Scarf

Materials

- Old Scarf
- Wooden Picture Frames
- Scissors

Directions

1. Take your old photo frames and lay them on your old scarf. Measure the outline of your photo frame onto the scarf.

2. Cut around the outline, and place the scarf cut-out into the photo frames.

3. Do this for as many photo frames as you want. Arrange them in any pattern you would like, when you hang them on your wall.

81. T-Shirt Apron

Materials

- Scissors
- Sewing machine
- Old shirt

Directions

1. Start by off the sleeves of your shirt at the seam. Now turn your shirt so the front is laying face down on your workspace. And make a cut from the bottom of the shirt all the way up to the collar, but do not cut into the collar of the shirt.

2. Now you need to cut around the collar of the shirt and remove all the fabric around it. Only leave the material that is in the front of the shirt. Mark one diagonal cut from the armpit to the top of the shoulder and then cut it off on each side in order to get a great look.

3. The last step involves doing ties for your apron. Use the sleeves you cut off to make some ties. If they are too small then you may use some ribbons.

82. Cloth Flowers

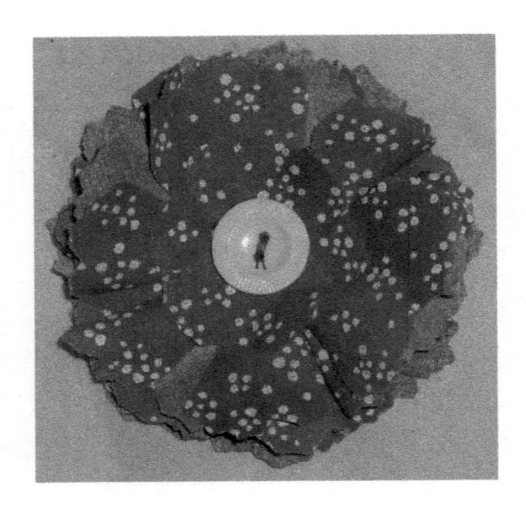

Materials

- Worn out clothes (you can use old scarf, cotton tops, skirt etc)
- Pair of scissors
- Designer scissors (these have wavy blades)
- Marker
- Hot glue
- Golden beads
- Metal wire
- Card board

Directions

1. You will have to assort the cloth according to colors. It will be best if you have some in green color.

2. Draw a flower petal and a leaf on the card board and cut them out to make the templates. You will use these templates to make the flower petals and leaves.

3. Place the leaf template on the green cloth pieces and mark with the marker pen. The same thing is to be done with the petal template using other colorful clothes.

4. Cut the leaves and petals out with the designer scissor. Use the sewing machine to stitch the leaf vein (make the main veins only) and also stitch the vein in the petals.

5. Cut the metal wire in 6-inch pieces and wrap the petals with the wire in the center in the shape of a flower. Use 8 petals to make a flower and add one leaf at the end. Fix the golden bead with hot glue in the middle of the flower.

83. Mail Bag

Materials

- Old cotton cloth
- Hot glue
- Scissors
- Marker pen
- Sewing machine and matching threads

Directions

1. Cut the cloth pieces into different shapes of designs to make decoration (you can make geometrical patterns or can make flower motifs).

2. Next take old cloth, and cut it into two squares. Then pin the edges, and sew together with a simple stitch to form the base of your bag

3. Then cut out 1-inch wide strips from the old cloth to make your straps and then attach them to the base of your bag. Then glue on the cloth decorations you made.

84. Laundry Bag

Materials

- Old hoodie sweat shirt
- Fabric paint
- Sewing machine and matching thread

Directions

1. Take your old hoodie, and hem the bottom closed. Cut off the sleeves and hem the openings closed.

2. Take your fabric paint and write "colors" or "whites" on the front of the hoodie Now you are finished the drawstring in the hoodie will allow you to open or close the bags.

85. Coaster

Materials

- Old cotton skirt
- Scissors
- Thread and needle

Directions

1. Start by cutting the cloth in long and narrow strips. Take 3 strips together to make a long braid. Tie the beginning and end of the braid tightly with thread.

2. Wrap the braids in circles (you can also make squares) and keep sewing each layer with the previous one. Keep wrapping and sewing till your coaster reaches the desired size.

86. Cat Tent Using Old T Shirts

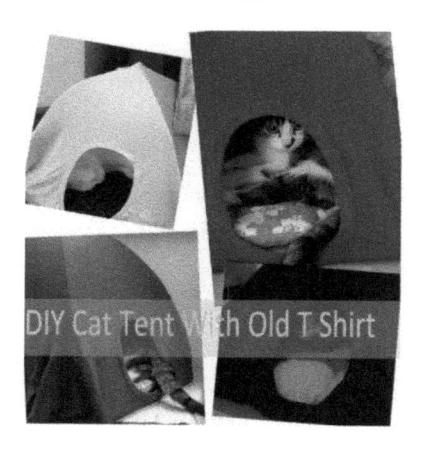

Materials

- Old t-shirt
- Old cushion
- 2 hangers
- Iron Wire and some strong paper

Directions

1. Start by straightening the 2 clothes hangers. Fix the middle of the hangers using iron wire and adjust the curvature of the hangers so that the room suits your cat. Put some cardboard under your cushion in order to enhance stability.

2. Put all things together and be careful with the ends of hangers (they are sharp and may hurt your kittens). Now put the old t-shirt to the bracket sleeve. Close any redundant holes and there you have it! Now get your cat in!

87. Table Napkins

Materials

- Old cotton cloth or old t-shirts
- Scissors
- Ruler
- ¼ inch wide satin or lace ribbon (few yards)
- Sewing machine and transparent thread

Directions

1. You will cut the cotton cloth in squares (10"x10" size will be best for table napkin). Make a set of 6 to 8 napkins with the same cloth.

2. Cut the lace ribbon in 10" pieces and sew them on all 4 edges of the napkins.

88. Table Cloth

Materials

- Old printed bed sheet
- Scissors
- Sewing machine and transparent thread
- Lace ribbon

Directions

1. Cut the cloth according to the measurements of your table. It must be bigger 1ft longer than the table on each side. So add 2ft to the length and width

2. Sew the lace ribbon along the four edges.

89. T-Shirt Quilt

Materials

- T-shirts with the collar and sleeves cut off
- Scissors
- Sewing machine
- Binding
- Quilt batting
- Large piece of cloth for backing the quilt

Directions

1. Take the t-shirts (make sure the collar and sleeves have been cut off) and sew them all together in whatever pattern you may like, but in the end, it must be a rectangle shape.

2. Take the material you will use for backing your quilt and cut it to the same size as the rectangle shape you made with the t-shirts.

3. Also put the quilt batting in between the t-shirt layer and the backing, and pin the three layers together. Sew the three layers together. Sew your binging along the edges of the quilt.

90. Christmas Wreath

Materials

- Wreath making ring
- Christmas cloth pieces
- Hot glue
- Scissors
- Decorative flowers motifs

Directions

1. Cut the cloth in long strips and wrap then around the wreath ring. Make stripes all over with different color. Stick the flowers all over with hot glue.

91. Denim Pocket Wall Hanger

Materials

- 10 pairs of old pants or skirts with back pockets
- Scraps of cloth
- Wall rack
- Sewing machine
- Ruler

Directions

1. Take your scrap cloth, and cut it into 9, 8x10inch squares, and sew them together into a square that is 3x3 rows. Then take your pants and cut out 9 pockets, then stitch the pockets onto the squares.

2. Fold over the top of the project 1 inch, and hem at the bottom of the fold, this way you can put your wall hanging rod through it like a curtain and hang it on the wall.

Kids Clothes, Toys, & More

92. Football for The Little Boy

Materials

- Old t-shirt are material scraps
- Needle and thread
- Sewing machine
- Scissors
- Synthetic fillers

Directions

1. Cut 3 football shape pieces of cloth, and sew them together, but leave a 3inch hole so you can full the football right side out and fill with stuffing.

2. Now fill the football with stuffing, make sure to pack the stuffing tight. Now stitch up the hole by hand.

3. Now take a few more scraps of material and cut out a circle and a stitch to make the stitches on the football, and stich these on the side of the football.

93. Baby Quilt

Materials

- Small pieces of scrap cloth
- Scissors
- Sewing machine
- Quilt batting
- Silk binding

Directions

1. Cut the cloth pieces in squares 4x4inch in measurement; sew them together to make a big rectangular cloth. You will have to make 2 sheets (for the front and back of the quilt.) You can make the quilt any size.

2. Pin the 2 layers and quilt batting, and sew them together. Add the silk binding to the outside of the quilt.

94. Adult Socks into Toddler Pants

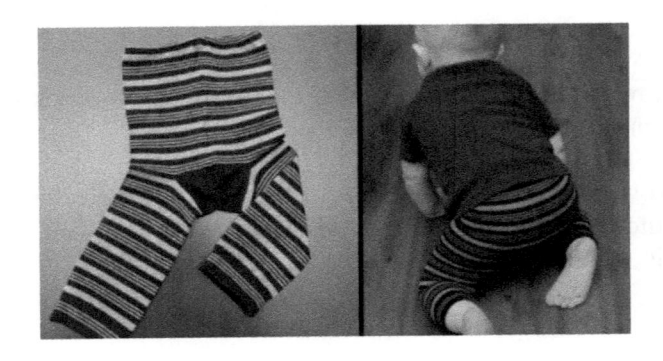

Materials

- One pair of adult socks and some elastic
- Scissors
- Sewing machine

Directions

1. Pick a pair of socks and cut the toe sections off. Split the socks along the center sole (where it's folded) from where you cut the toe section off all the way through the center of the heel section.

2. Turn one of the socks inside out and insert the other sock (right side out) inside the first sock. Line up the edges and sew or overlock along the seam (use a zigzag stitch). This will be the crotch seam so leave the top open (where you cut the toe off).

3. Next, sew the crotch seam using a zigzag stitch or overlock the elastic to the inside out upper edge of the pair of socks (the open edge). Fold the edge with the swimwear or standard braided elastic to the inside and zigzag along the edge to create a nice neat finished edge. That's it!

95. Children's Hat made from Old Sweaters

Materials

- Sweater (Preferably one that has a ribbing along the bottom) to give you the nice snug brim for your hat)
- Scissors
- Sewing machine
- Flower motif, buttons, pom poms, or bows

Directions

1. Line up the bottom edge of your sweater (back and front) and nicely cut out a rounded hat shape. Be sure to make it tall enough so as to cover the head and then come down to cover the ears. Place both hat pieces together and stitch along the curve of your hat.

2. Either sew another straight stitch close to the first one or do a zigzag stitch. Note that sometimes zigzag stitches on woven material can stretch out. Therefore, increase the stitch length so that it jumps over more fabric. Otherwise, you may want to stick to an additional straight stitch.

3. Trim the excess edges, if necessary. Attach any flower motifs you have or decorations to the hat. Turn your hat right side out, and you 're done!

96. Baby Leg Warmers from An Old Sweater

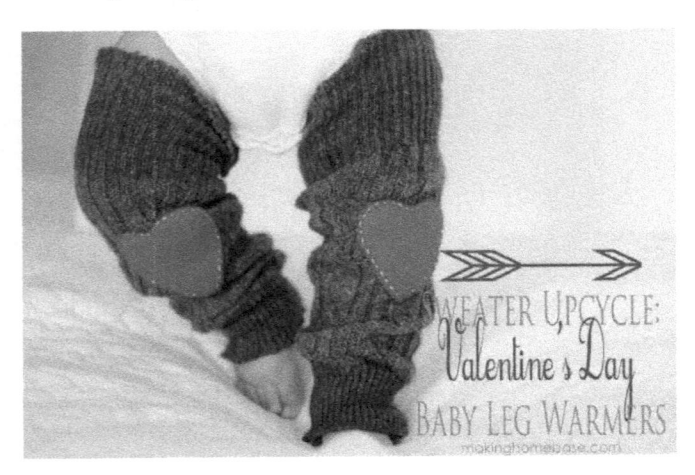

Materials

- Old sweater
- Sewing machine
- Motif heart

Directions

1. Cut the sleeves off from and old sweater, and cut up the side seam.

2. Take in the seam of the sweater to fit around your baby's legs.

3. Hem the cut edge of the sweater. Iron on your heart motif

97. T-Shirt to A Toddler Dress

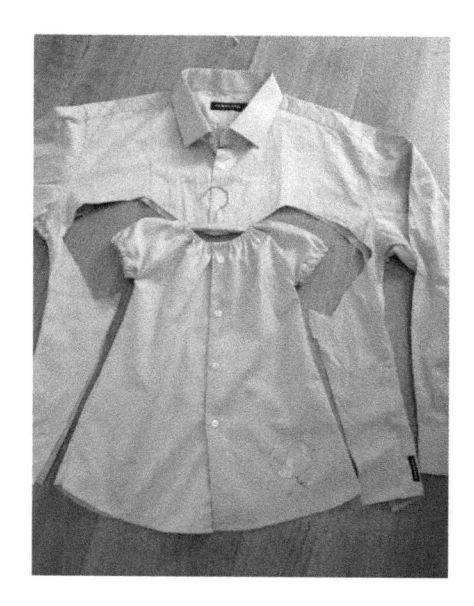

Materials

- Pins
- Sewing machine
- Chalk
- Old dress or t-shirt
- Iron on decoration or flower motif

Directions

1. One of the easiest ways to figure out the pattern is to one of your old toddler dresses as a pattern.

2. Trace around the dress on one side, giving about 1-inch buffer for the seams. Continue with folding the shirt in half and pin the edges to be easier for you.

3. Cut the along the marked lines and unfold it. Turn it inside out. You can also use overcasting stitch to prevent fraying and continue sewing. Now turn the t-shirt right side out. By now it should look like a dress. Attach any decorations or motifs to the dress.

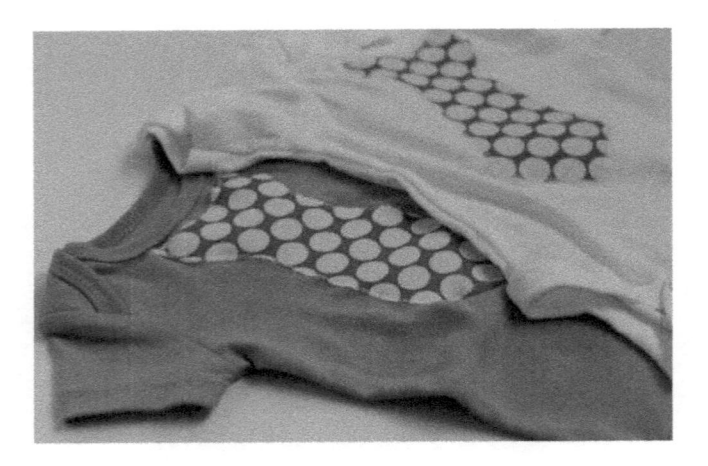

98. Tie Onesie

Materials

- Tie stencil
- Scraps of fabric
- An old plain onesie or T-shirt

Directions

1. Trace the tie pattern onto the t-shirt or onesie. Cut out the backing and iron it on.

2. Next, cut out the tie shape and iron it onto the t-shirt or onesie. Zigzag stitch all around the tie.

99. Kids' Art Apron from A Dishtowel

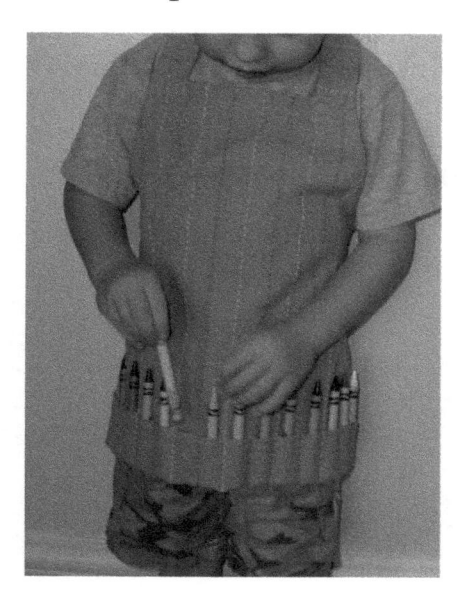

Materials

- Box of crayons
- Dish towel (prewashed)

Directions

1. Cut 2 inches off each long side of the dishtowel. These will be the ties. Cut off 2 inches again off one short side of the dish towel. This will be the neck strap.

2. Next, hem the cut side of each strip, turning them twice for a nicer finished edge. You can measure if you like or just eyeball it!

3. Figure out the length you need for the apron and add three inches. This is the length you'll need to cut the towel. Now cut from the same edge you cut the neck strap so that you'll still have 1 hemmed edge on the towel. Then cut out the armholes.

4. Hem all the unfinished sides and most importantly, turn the 3 raw sides to the opposite side the current hem is on. That way, the hem will be on the front of the apron when you turn the pocket up. Do this for the two sides first before the top edge with a larger hem.

5. Fold the pocket up 2 inches and mark every one inch to create the crayon pockets. Next, attach the straps and fill it up with crayons. Tie it on your little one and let the art fun begin!

100. Superhero's Cape for Kids

Materials

- Old t-shirt
- Scissors
- Felt scraps
- Glitter paint

Directions

1. Use a pair of scissors to cut the side of each t-shirt around the front side of the neck hole and across the back of the arms to create an awesome basic cape shape.

2. Create an additional mask and bands using the actual arms you just cut from the old t-shirt. You will also need to cut the eyes holes using the scissors and embellish.

3. Use a few pieces of felt to create lightning bolts and circles at the back and glitter paint to adorn each cape with your kid's name.

4. Optional: Add a Velcro strip to the front of the neckband for easy removal. All done!

Conclusion

Reusing old clothes is good for the environment and you can create extraordinary items for your home and personal use.

Most of the materials you will need to make these projects are generally available at home, and you will just have to buy certain things like the matching ribbons, synthetic fillers and decorating beads.

I hope you enjoyed this 4th edition, the new crafts that were added, and the adjustments to the old crafts. When adding crafts and revising this book I took into consideration a lot of the comments left in amazon.

I care how my fans feel about my books, and feel free to leave a comment about the new and revised "Upcycling Crafts." I would love to hear your feedback.

Last Chance to Get YOUR Bonus!

FOR A LIMITED TIME ONLY – Get my best-selling book "DIY Crafts: The 100 Most Popular Crafts & Projects That Make Your Life Easier" absolutely FREE!

Readers who have downloaded the bonus book as well have seen the greatest changes in their crafting abilities and have expanded their repertoire of crafts – so it is *highly recommended* to get this bonus book today!

Get your free copy at:

ArtsCraftsAndMore.com/Bonus

Final Words

Thank you for downloading this book!

I really hope that you have been inspired to create your own projects and that you will have a lot of fun crafting.

I do hope that you and your family have found lots of ways to fill lazy afternoons or rainy days in a more fun way.

If you have enjoyed this book and would like to share your positive thoughts, could you please take 30 seconds of your time to go back and give me a review on my Amazon book page!

I really appreciate these reviews because I like to know what people have thought about the book.

Again, thank you and have fun crafting!

Disclaimer

No Warranties: The authors and publishers don't guarantee or warrant the quality, accuracy, completeness, timeliness, appropriateness or suitability of the information in this book, or of any product or services referenced by this site.

The information in this site is provided on an "as is" basis and the authors and publishers make no representations or warranties of any kind with respect to this information. This site may contain inaccuracies, typographical errors, or other errors.

Liability Disclaimer: The publishers, authors, and other parties involved in the creation, production, provision of information, or delivery of this site specifically disclaim any responsibility, and shall not be held liable for any damages, claims, injuries, losses, liabilities, costs, or obligations including any direct, indirect, special, incidental, or consequences damages (collectively known as "Damages") whatsoever and howsoever caused, arising out of, or in connection with the use or misuse of the site and the information contained within it, whether such Damages arise in contract, tort, negligence, equity, statute law, or by way of other legal theory.

Lightning Source UK Ltd.
Milton Keynes UK
UKHW011200170520
363415UK00006B/1273